Hot or Cold?

Barbara L. Webb

rourkeeducationalmedia.com

 Teacher Notes available at rem4teachers.com

www.rourkeeducationalmedia.com

PHOTO CREDITS: Cover: © Dmitry Pichugin, © Goinyk Volodymyr; Title page: © kristian sekulic; page 3: © Gerville Hall, © majana; page 4: © Beboy_ltd; page 4, 5: © johnnylemonseed; page 5: © Bruce Smith; page 6: © Sean Randall; page 7: © Kevin Drinkall; page 8: © Eric Simard; page 9, 12, 14, 16, 18-21:© Renee Brady; page 10: © Jeeragone Inrut; page 11: © Tom Young; page 13: water slide; page 14: © Moodboard, © sean boggs, ; page 15: © Shelly Au; page 17: © Marzanna Syncerz; page 20: © Rhienna Cutler; page 22: © VisualField, © david franklin; page 22: © Jitalia17, © penguenstok

Edited by Precious McKenzie

Cover design by Teri Intzegian
Interior design by Renee Brady

Library of Congress PCN Data

Hot or Cold? / Barbara L. Webb
(Little World Math Concepts)
ISBN 978-1-61810-069-6 (hard cover)(alk. paper)
ISBN 978-1-61810-202-7 (soft cover)
Library of Congress Control Number: 2011944366

Rourke Educational Media
Printed in the United States of America,
North Mankato, Minnesota

rourkeeducationalmedia.com
customerservice@rourkeeducationalmedia.com • PO Box 643328 Vero Beach, Florida 32964

Hot or cold?

How do you know?

Hot

Cold

The desert is hot.

The mountain is cold.

To be exact, we use degrees to measure temperature.

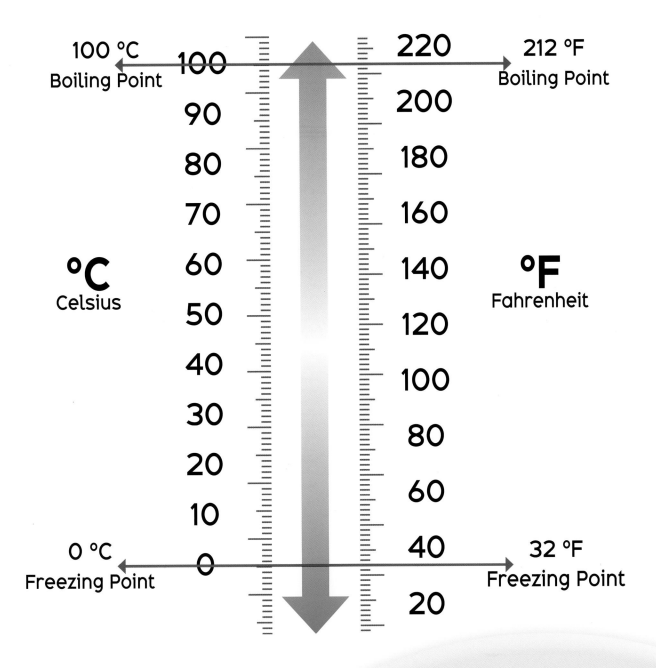

100 °C
Boiling Point

212 °F
Boiling Point

100

220

90

200

80

180

70

160

°C
Celsius

60

140

°F
Fahrenheit

50

120

40

100

30

80

20

60

10

40

0 °C
Freezing Point

0

32 °F
Freezing Point

20

A thermometer is the tool we use

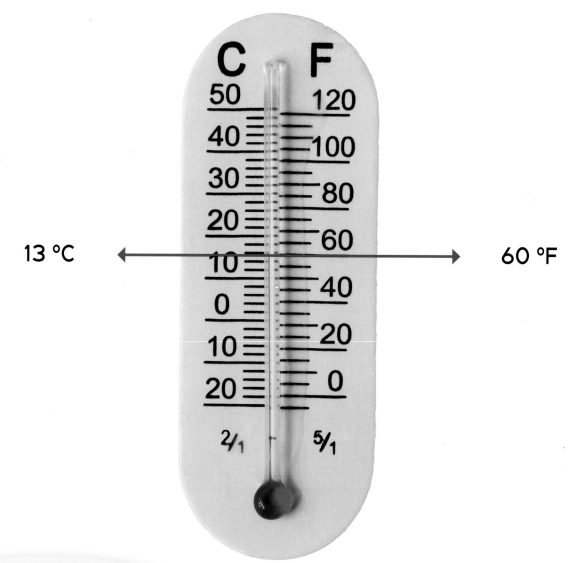

13 °C ← → 60 °F

to know the kind of coat to choose.

If the red line is long and tall, you might not need a coat at all!

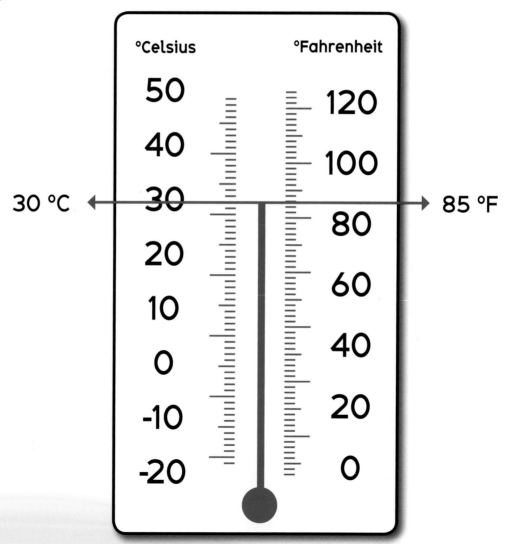

The higher the number of degrees, the hotter it feels to you and me.

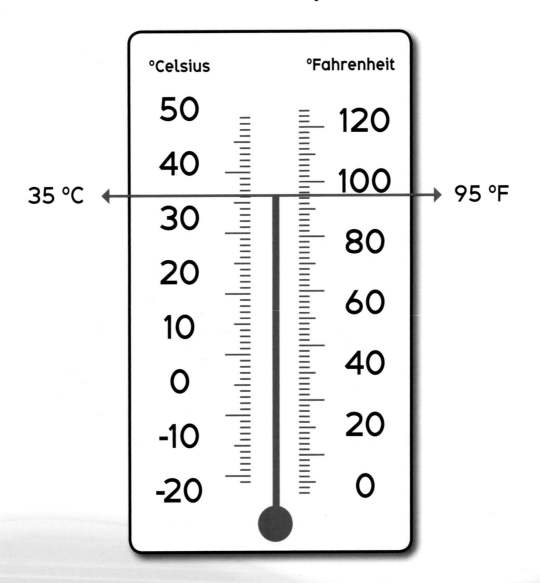

°Celsius

°Fahrenheit

50

40

35 °C ← → 95 °F

30

20

10

0

-10

-20

120

100

80

60

40

20

0

If the red line falls lower, the colder it feels to you and me.

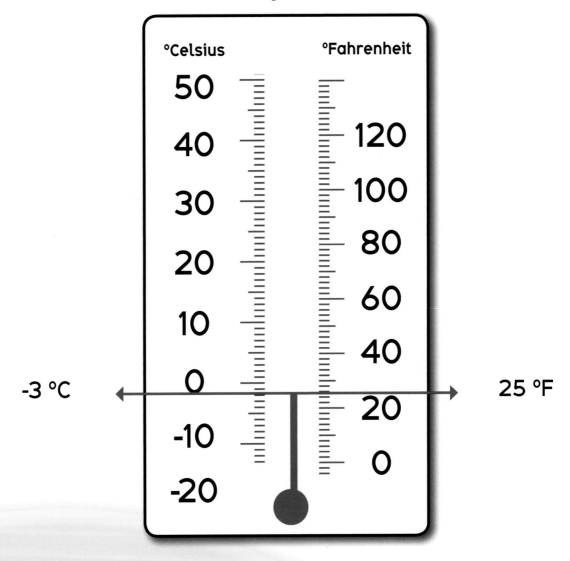

-3 °C

25 °F

Brrr!

Look at these thermometers.

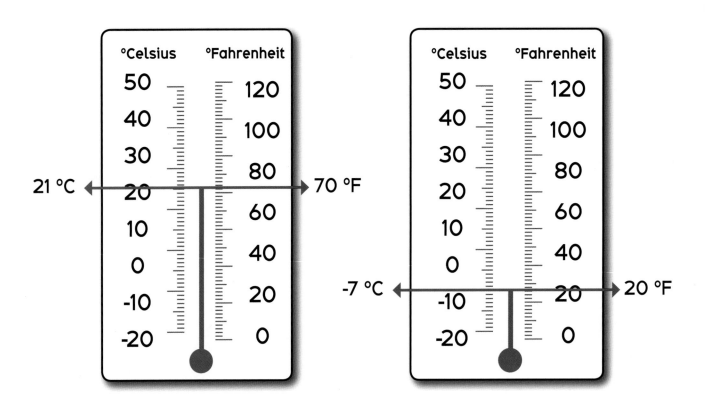

Which shows the cold, warm, and hot day?

Did you get it right?

cold

°Celsius | °Fahrenheit

50 — 120
40 — 100
30 — 80
20 — 60
10 —
0 — 40
-7 °C ← → 20 °F
-10 — 20
-20 — 0

warm

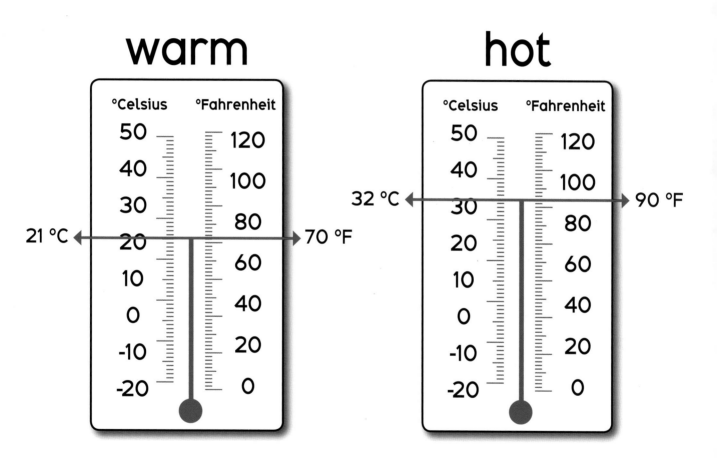

°Celsius

°Fahrenheit

°Celsius	°Fahrenheit
50	120
40	100
30	80
20	60
10	40
0	20
-10	0
-20	

21 °C ← → 70 °F

hot

°Celsius

°Fahrenheit

32 °C ← → 90 °F

Telling temperature is such fun. Now show me what to wear!

cold

°Celsius °Fahrenheit

50 — 120
40 — 100
30 — 80
20 — 60
10 — 40
0 —
-7 °C ← | → 20 °F
-10 — 20
-20 — 0

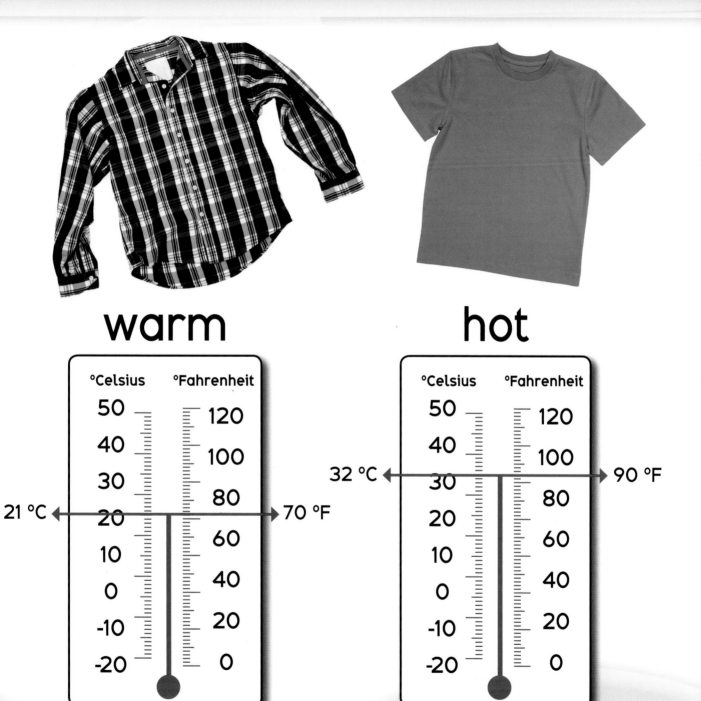

warm

hot

°Celsius °Fahrenheit

21 °C → 70 °F

32 °C → 90 °F

23

Index

Websites

www.mathsisfun.com/measure/thermometer.html

www.weatherwizkids.com/weather-temperature.htm

www.sproutonline.com/currentsite/firesafety/hotncold.php

About the Author

Barbara Webb lives in Chicago where the weather is sometimes very hot and sometimes very cold. She is the author of ten books on math, science, and history for kids.

Ask The Author!
www.rem4students.com